AF496578
TUDOR
1485-1603
STUART
1603-1714
GEORGIAN
1714-1837
VICTORIAN
1837-1901
MODERN TIMES
1902-NOW

children's HISTORY of WINDSOR

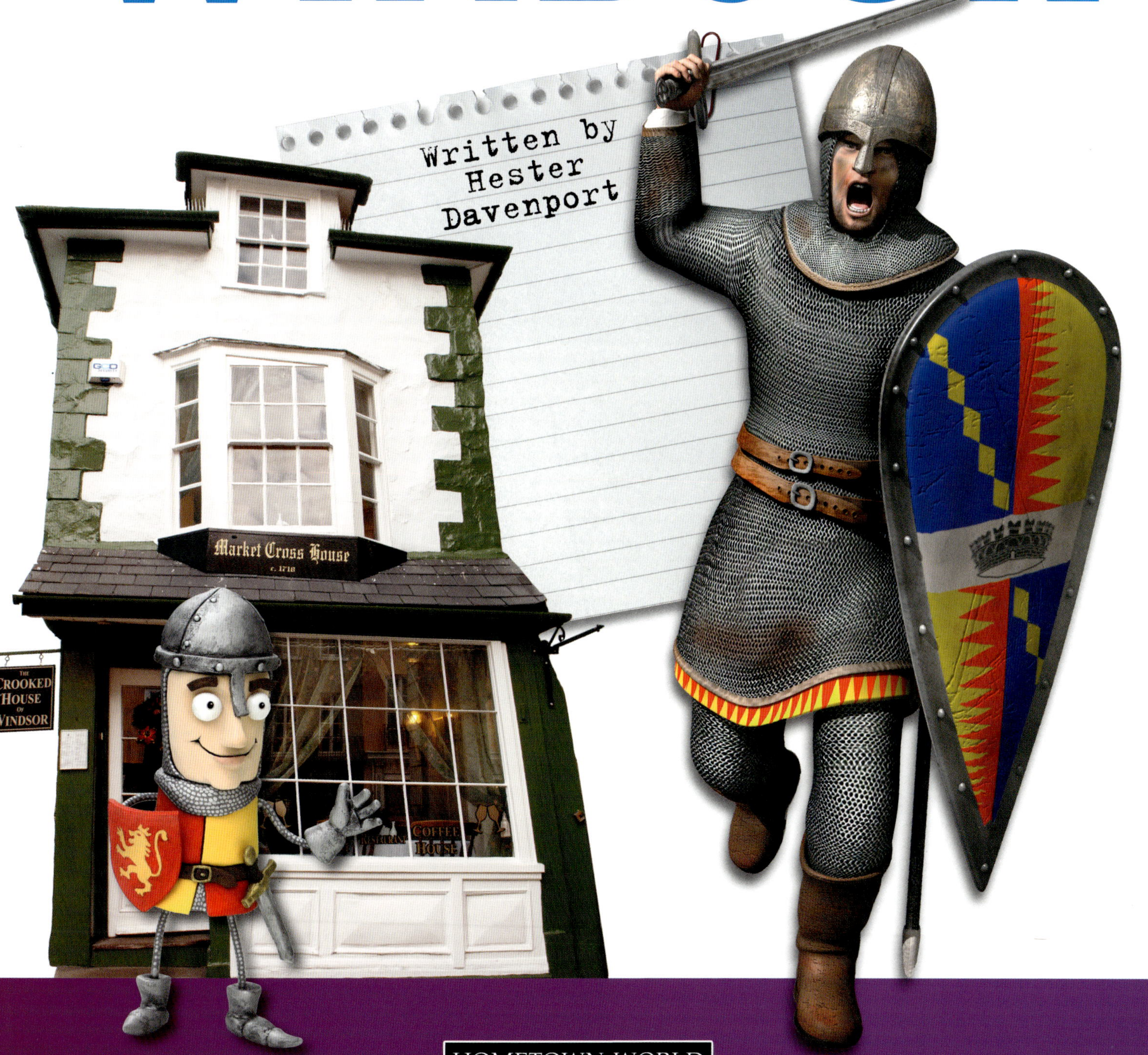

HOMETOWN WORLD

How well do you know your town?

Have you ever wondered what it would have been like living in Windsor when the Romans arrived? What about rubbing shoulders with the finest people in the land at the castle? This book will uncover the important and exciting things that happened in your town.

Want to hear the other good bits? You will love this book! An expert team has worked on it to make sure it's fun and informative. So what are you waiting for? Peel back the pages and be amazed at what happened in your town.

THE FACTS

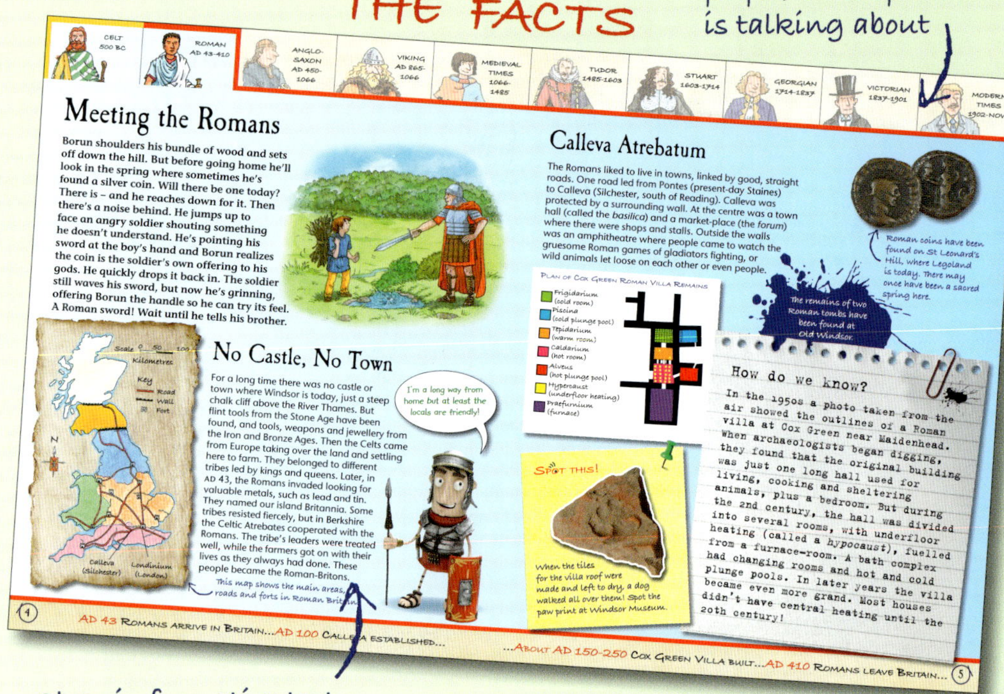

Timeline shows which period (dates and people) each spread is talking about

Clear informative text

Hometown facts to amaze you!

THE EVIDENCE

A King at Kingsbury

Saxon Manor

Norman Invasion

William the Conqueror

How do we know?

Intriguing old photos

'Spot this!' game with hints on something to find in your town

Each period in the book ends with a summary explaining how we know about the past

Go back in time to read what it was like for children growing up in Windsor

VIKING
MEDIEVAL TIMES
TUDOR
STUART
GEORGIAN
VICTORIAN
MODERN TIMES
AD 800
AD 900
1000
1100
1200
1300
1400
1500
1600
1700
1800
1900
2000

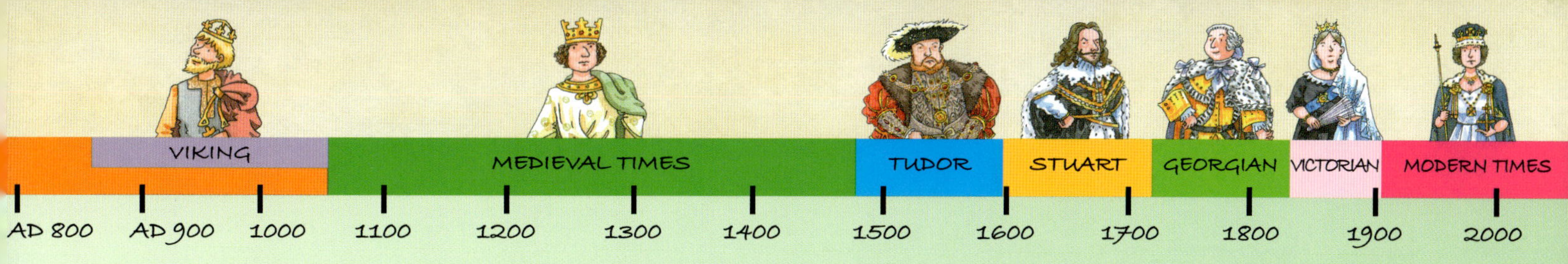

Contents

Meeting the Romans

Borun shoulders his bundle of wood and sets off down the hill. But before going home he'll look in the spring where sometimes he's found a silver coin. Will there be one today? There is – and he reaches down for it. Then there's a noise behind. He jumps up to face an angry soldier shouting something he doesn't understand. He's pointing his sword at the boy's hand and Borun realizes the coin is the soldier's own offering to his gods. He quickly drops it back in. The soldier still waves his sword, but now he's grinning, offering Borun the handle so he can try its feel. A Roman sword! Wait until he tells his brother.

No Castle, No Town

For a long time there was no castle or town where Windsor is today, just a steep chalk cliff above the River Thames. But flint tools from the Stone Age have been found, and tools, weapons and jewellery from the Iron and Bronze Ages. Then the Celts came from Europe taking over the land and settling here to farm. They belonged to different tribes led by kings and queens. Later, in AD 43, the Romans invaded looking for valuable metals, such as lead and tin. They named our island Britannia. Some tribes resisted fiercely, but in Berkshire the Celtic Atrebates cooperated with the Romans. The tribe's leaders were treated well, while the farmers got on with their lives as they always had done. These people became the Roman-Britons.

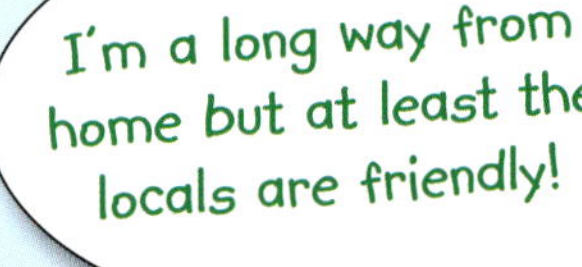

This map shows the main areas, roads and forts in Roman Britain.

AD 43 ROMANS ARRIVE IN BRITAIN...AD 100 CALLEVA ESTABLISHED...

Calleva Atrebatum

The Romans liked to live in towns linked by good, straight roads. One road led from Pontes (present-day Staines) to Calleva (Silchester, south of Reading). Calleva was protected by a surrounding wall. At the centre was a town hall (called the *basilica*) and a market-place (the *forum*) where there were shops and stalls. Outside the walls was an amphitheatre where people came to watch the gruesome Roman games of gladiators fighting, or wild animals let loose on each other or even people.

Roman coins have been found on St Leonard's Hill, where Legoland is today. There may once have been a sacred spring here.

The remains of two Roman tombs have been found at Old Windsor.

PLAN OF COX GREEN ROMAN VILLA REMAINS

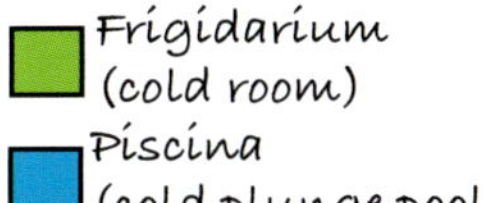

How do we know?

In the 1950s a photo taken from the air showed the outlines of a Roman villa at Cox Green near Maidenhead. When archaeologists began digging, they found that the original building was just one long hall used for living, cooking and sheltering animals, plus a bedroom. But during the 2nd century, the hall was divided into several rooms, with underfloor heating (called a *hypocaust*), fuelled from a furnace-room. A bath complex had changing rooms and hot and cold plunge pools. In later years the villa became even more grand. Most houses didn't have central heating until the 20th century!

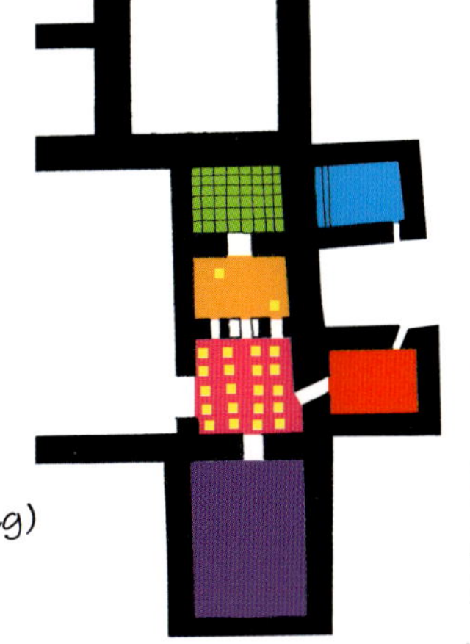

SPOT THIS!

When the tiles for the villa roof were made and left to dry, a dog walked all over them! Spot the paw print at Windsor Museum.

A King at Kingsbury

An excited crowd hurries to the palace. The king, famed for his wisdom and holiness, is to appear wearing his crown. People want to see him, though in his eagerness one man will regret that on the way he loses a tiny ornament from his knife-handle. They all crush inside and there's a hush as King Edward comes through an archway, cross in hand and golden crown glinting over his snow-white hair.

Saxon Manor

After the Romans left in AD 410, Angles, Saxons and Jutes invaded Britain from Europe. The first settlers were pagans who worshipped many different gods. From around AD 600 the Anglo-Saxons became Christians, building churches and monasteries. At that time Berkshire was part of the kingdom of Wessex.

In the 9th century there were new invaders, fierce Vikings from Scandinavia, who raided along the River Thames as far as Reading. But after King Alfred the Great defeated the Vikings the kingdoms were united as Angleland. Life wasn't always peaceful even then, but there were settlements at Dedworth and Wraysbury and a manor at Clewer.

A royal manor grew up near the river at Kingsbury, now known as Old Windsor. There was good hunting and fishing there, and abundant wood from the forest, as well as easy access by river. When Edward the Confessor came to the throne in 1042, he held Great Councils at the royal manor in Old Windsor.

This Saxon bronze ornament shaped like a dog's head is known as the 'Kingsbury Beast'. It is just 2.5 cm long. We have shown it larger. It may have come from a knife-handle.

Norman Invasion

When King Edward the Confessor died in 1066 a powerful earl called Harold Godwinson had himself crowned king. But Duke William of Normandy declared that he had been promised the throne. He invaded with his army, killed Harold, and defeated the Saxons at the Battle of Hastings. He became known as William the Conqueror.

William the Conqueror

Emma lives in Wraysbury, across the river from Kingsbury. In the imaginary account below, she tells how she went to a 'crown-wearing' where the king appeared among the people wearing his crown.

Can you spot this Saxon bone comb which was dug up at Wraysbury? Look for it in the Museum.

The 'crown-wearing' was when the king appeared before his people wearing his crown.

It was so exciting! I wore my new blue kirtle. Mother combed my hair until it shone, she said, like gold. Then we took a boat across the river. The King's hall was crowded and it was hard to see anything, but when Father lifted me up I saw King Edward in his golden crown. Then there was a noise at the door. The attendants were trying to keep someone out but people shouted 'Let him in!' The man, called Wulfrin, couldn't see properly and the crowd helped him make his way to the King. The King told the priest to bring holy water from the church, then he gently sponged Wulfrin's eyes, while saying a prayer. It went very quiet until suddenly Wulfrin cried out 'I see you, O King!' Everybody cheered and hugged each other. It was awesome!

How do we know?

The monk, William of Malmesbury, wrote an account of Wulfrin's miracle cure.

We can also tell a great deal from excavations. No one knew where Kingsbury was until 1951 when workmen in Old Windsor unearthed a lot of Saxon objects near the church, including the Saxon ornament known as the Kingsbury Beast. Archaeologists identified the site as Kingsbury. They found a canal leading to a water-mill and the remains of houses, though not the royal palace which may lie beneath the churchyard.

Castle and Town

Bend, shovel up soil, lift, tip it in baskets for others to take to the growing mound. Wilf's back aches. He hears picks thudding into the earth to loosen it, sawing and hammering as supports are built for the sides of the deepening moat. Wilf's one of an army of men brought in to build the new king's castle and he's glad to have food and shelter, though it's hard work. There's a shout as the Norman in charge notices him leaning on his shovel. He waves to show he's sorry and starts again. Bend, shovel, lift, tip.

When the Round Tower was first built it was much lower than it is today.

The Conqueror

The chalk cliff at Windsor was the perfect place for a castle – easy to defend, impressive and near good hunting forest. King William brought new motte-and-bailey castle-building methods from Normandy. The motte was a mound of soil surrounded by a moat. When the soil was firm, a wooden keep was built on top. The bailey was a fenced courtyard around the keep. At Windsor there were two baileys – the Upper Ward with the royal apartments, and the Lower Ward for soldiers, workmen and servants. In time the castle's wooden walls and buildings were replaced with stone and, in 1110, William's son, King Henry I, held his court for the first time in 'New Windsor'.

The Town Takes Shape

The castle provided lots of work, attracting people from Old Windsor to live there, at first in the Lower Ward. Timber houses clustered below the walls, and an island of little streets developed outside the main gate. A church was built and a wooden bridge led over the river to Eton. New Windsor grew and, in 1277, King Edward I granted the town a charter, allowing it to manage its own affairs.

Magna Carta

William's great-great-grandson, King John, was very unpopular. His rule was so unjust that the nobles rebelled and demanded reforms. John was forced to ride 5 kilometres from the castle to meet them at Runnymede where, on 15th June, 1215 his seal was set on Magna Carta. It had 63 clauses, the most important being that nobody was to be imprisoned except by the law of the land. But King John soon broke his promises.

The Magna Carta was sealed at Runnymede, midway between the king in Windsor and the barons in Staines. This memorial marks the spot today.

King John's seal.

King John seals the Magna Carta, a charter that granted the first freedoms to the English nobility.

Henry III was crowned with a simple gold band because the royal crown was lost at sea.

The Town Takes a Battering

The angry barons invited Prince Louis of France to become king instead of John. Much of southern England was eventually conquered and Windsor Castle was under siege. Siege-weapons hurled great stones at the walls. Much damage was done to the town as well as the castle, and at Old Windsor the French destroyed the church. At last, after three months, the attackers withdrew, and it was not long afterwards that John died and was succeeded by his nine-year-old son, Henry III.

Peascod Street used to lead to pea fields at Clewer. A 'peascod' is an Anglo-Saxon name for a pea pod. Can you spot this Norman carving on the font in St Andrew's Church?

Jousting!

Hooves drum as two knights, their visors down, long lances at the ready, ride along the lists towards each other. With his shield, one knight fends off the other's lance while dealing his opponent such a powerful blow that the opponent crashes to the ground. The victor rides on to cheers while the fallen knight lies there, his armour too heavy for him to get up unaided. He's badly bruised but there is some honour in being beaten by the King himself.

Sir William Montagu, 1st Earl of Salisbury, died from his wounds following the tournament of 1344.

The Order of the Garter emblem hangs above a doorway at Windsor Castle.

The Great Tournament

King Edward III, born at Windsor, loved the sport of jousting. In 1344 he summoned all the young knights of England to the castle for a tournament. There was feasting and merry-making but on the last day a solemn announcement: the King, wearing his crown, said that he intended to found a great order of knights, to be like the legendary King Arthur and his Round Table.

The Order of the Garter

The Order of the Garter was created in 1348. It was, and still is, the most important chivalric order in England. Its sign is a garter embroidered with the motto 'Honi soit qui mal y pense' (Evil be to him who evil thinks), worn by men on the leg and by women on the arm. Twenty-four knights were appointed in addition to the King and his son: that number remains the same today. The King also declared that there would be an annual service in St George's Chapel. The garter ceremony and procession still takes place every June in Windsor Castle.

The Garter Feast

A grand feast was held on 23rd April, St George's Day, each year. Meat was served on trenchers – thick slices of bread – and eaten with your fingers. Food was served by pages while minstrels played, and jugglers and acrobats entertained the knights and their ladies.

Geoffrey Chaucer, who wrote *The Canterbury Tales*, was a young pageboy to the Countess of Ulster, wife of Edward III's son Lionel. Chaucer entertained the court with his stories.

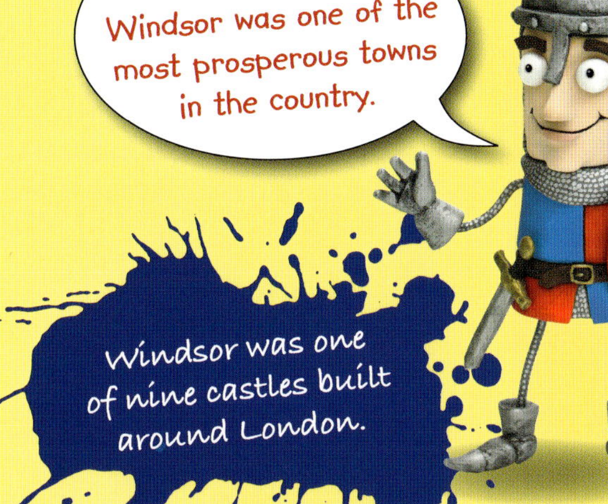

Eton and St George's Chapel

Eton College was established by King Henry VI in 1440 as a free school for 70 boys from noble but poor families. But he lost his throne in the Wars of the Roses to King Edward IV. Edward rebuilt St George's Chapel, perhaps to rival the magnificence of Henry's Eton College Chapel.

Spot this!

Can you spot the Windsor Royal Beasts – heraldic statues of animals representing the royal family through the ages? Look up at the roof of St George's Chapel.

How do we know?

Tournaments were an important part of a knight's education, training him for war. There are many accounts of chivalry, such as Chaucer's *The Knight's Tale*, one of his 'Canterbury Tales'. Although he was not a noble, his father served King Edward III and Chaucer had a knight's education. The Countess of Ulster's household accounts, found lining a book, show that in April 1357 she bought a paltock (short jacket) for 'Galfrido Chaucer', plus some shoes and red and black hose (tights). Chaucer served the royal court all his life, ending as Clerk of the Works, which made him responsible for royal buildings such as St George's.

Dangerous Times

Loud knocking brings John Marbeck to his door. All day there have been rumours of arrests of heretics.

'The soldiers are coming!' warns a friend. 'Save yourself, John.' The noise has woken Mistress Marbeck, who peers anxiously through the window nursing her baby.

'The King is just and will not let harm befall me,' her husband tells her. Another knock at the door, louder this time. Two men are there with a party of soldiers.

'John Marbeck?' demands one. 'We have a commission from the King to search your house for unlawful books.' The soldiers lead him roughly away.

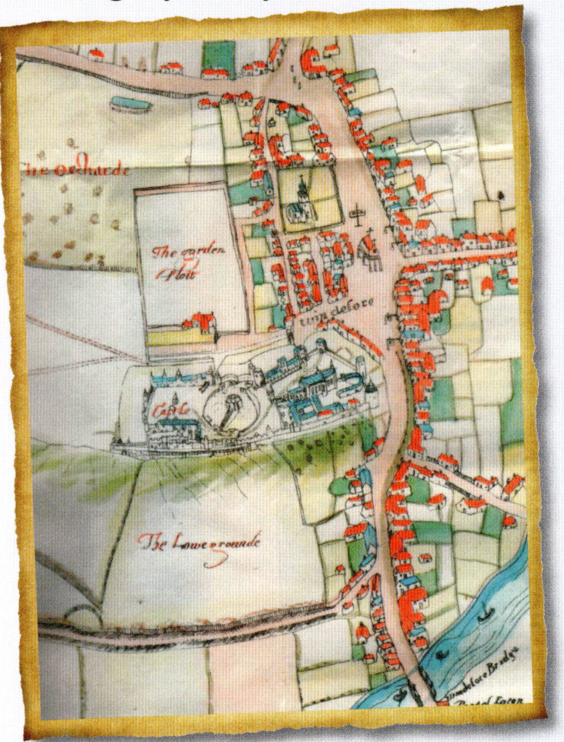

John Norden made this map of Windsor in 1607. Can you see the main street, castle and pillory in the market square?

Henry VIII

Religion was a dangerous subject when Henry VIII was king. Around 1530, Henry fell out with the Catholic pope over his divorce from the queen, Catherine of Aragon. First he declared himself head of the Church of England. Later, he passed a law which meant that everyone had to accept Catholic ideas or risk being accused of being a 'heretic'. Heretics were punished by being tied to a stake and burnt alive. In Windsor three men suffered this terrible fate.

Petty criminals were punished by being locked in the town pillory. People passing by would shout insults or throw rotten fruit and vegetables at them.

...*1509* Henry VIII crowned...*1543* Windsor Martyrs burned...

The Windsor Martyrs

In 1543, John Marbeck, Robert Testwood, Henry Filmer, Anthony Pierson and Robert Bennett were arrested. All were tried on suspicion of being heretics, except Robert Bennett who was ill. The evidence was weak, but it was enough to condemn a man if he had a book in his house of which the church disapproved. The brother of Henry Filmer, a tailor, swore he'd heard Henry joking about the holy sacrament, though it was widely believed he'd been paid to say so. The jury was made up from men who depended on the church for their living so, not surprisingly, they found the men guilty. John Marbeck, a musician at St George's, was at the last moment pardoned by the King, and Robert Bennett was later pardoned too. But Testwood, Filmer and Pierson were burned to death. Roads in West Windsor are named after the martyrs.

The Windsor martyrs were burned to death near where the Riverside Station is today.

There was no rubbish collection then so people threw it into the street or the river.

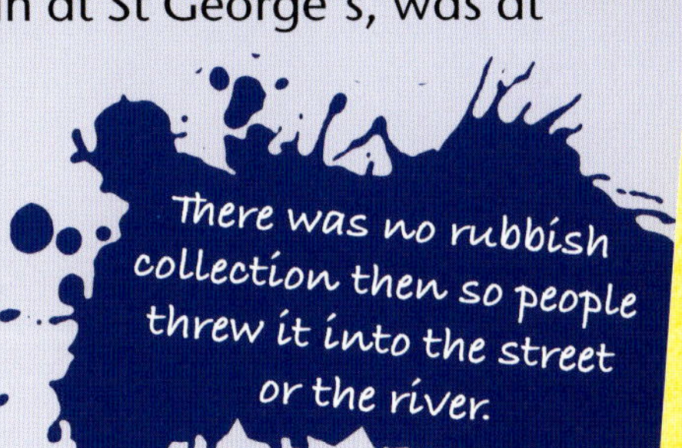

Can you spot this plaque which commemorates the three brave martyrs. Look at the bottom of Thames Street by the George V memorial.

The Windsor Witches

Ordinary people worried more about witches than heretics. Many people believed that witches could contact the devil by using a cat or other pet as a messenger. These animals were called 'familiars'. Sadly, some women really believed they had such powers. In 1574, while Elizabeth I was queen, Elizabeth Style confessed to being a witch, claiming to have brought about several deaths, including that of Richard Gallis, the Windsor mayor. Her familiar was a pet rat called Philip. She named other witches – Mother Devell who had a black cat called Jill, Mother Margaret with a kitten called Jenny, and Mother Dutton who kept a pet toad in her herb garden. They were all very poor women, but they were tried for witchcraft, and since Elizabeth Style described their 'crimes' in detail all four were hanged.

This is an imaginary account by Robin, a serving-boy at the Garter Inn. He writes about an interesting meeting he's had.

Master Shakespeare from the London playhouse is staying at the Garter! Today he came in very wet from a downpour of rain and ordered a flagon of ale. 'And put a toast in it, to warm me up!' So I heated the iron to red-hot then plunged it in his drink where it sizzled and fizzed. Master Shakespeare told me to sit by him on the high-backed settle seat while he drank. 'Do you like your schooling?' he asked. 'I hate Latin,' I said, 'but I hate the master's cane more, so I try to learn my *hic, haec, hocs*.' He laughed and said his school days were the same. He said he was going to write a play for Queen Elizabeth, and set it in Windsor, so he'd been exploring until he got caught in the rain. He'd sheltered under a big oak tree. 'Herne's Oak?' I asked. 'What's that?' he said. I told him the story of Herne the Hunter, keeper of the king's deer until he lost the king's favour and hanged himself from the oak tree. Now he haunts the park. 'Have you seen him?' asked Master Shakespeare. 'Not me,' I said, 'I keep away from that old oak.' He asked my name, and then said 'Robin – I'll remember that.'

[Herne's Oak — Sixty years since.]

The original Herne's Oak was cut down in the early 1800s. Edward VII planted a new one in 1906.

This stained glass picture of Falstaff is on the stairs at the Hart and Garter Hotel.

This is the story of 'The Merry Wives of Windsor', written by William Shakespeare around 1597.

A fat, penniless knight, called Sir John Falstaff, stays at the Garter Inn with his servant-boy Robin. He hopes to charm Mistress Ford and Mistress Page so that he can get their husbands' money. When he writes them identical love-letters, they decide to teach him a lesson. They play tricks on him, firstly getting him to hide from Mistress Ford's husband in a laundry basket, which her servants then tip in the Thames near Datchet. At the end of the play the women persuade him to meet them in the park at midnight, disguised as Herne the Hunter to scare off onlookers. But it's Falstaff who's scared when 'fairies' appear to pinch and poke him. In fact they're local children and Falstaff realizes he's been made a fool of. But the play ends in forgiveness and friendship.

How do we know?

Maps can tell us a lot about how the town has changed over time. John Norden's map shows the same main streets as today, the church and the market house with the pillory behind.

Detailed information about the Windsor Martyrs, supplied by the survivor John Marbeck, is recorded in *Foxe's Book of Martyrs*. It was published in 1563 and contained accounts of all those burned as heretics in the reigns of Henry VIII and Mary I. Pamphlets written at the time tell the story of the Windsor Witches.

There's no clear evidence that Shakespeare was ever in Windsor, but the details in his play of the town and its surroundings suggest that he must have visited. He probably wrote it in 1597 when Queen Elizabeth installed Sir George Hunsdon, Lord Chamberlain and patron of Shakespeare's theatre company, as a Garter Knight in St George's Chapel.

The King is Dead

It's 9th February, 1649. Snow falls on the black velvet pall which covers the coffin of the executed king, and on the heads of the soldiers who carry it into the Chapel. Parliament has forbidden any service or prayers to be said, so it is lowered silently into a vault. When the covering stone slabs are replaced nothing will show that this is the grave of King Charles I.

Charles I's coffin was placed beside Henry VIII's. Its whereabouts remained unknown for a long time.

Civil War

In 1642 civil war broke out. Parliament, led by Oliver Cromwell, did not like the way the king, Charles I, ruled or the way he treated people who criticized him. Parliamentary troops took over Windsor Castle. The dashing Royalist Prince Rupert tried to retake the castle but, though his guns damaged the town, the castle walls held firm.

Windsor citizens at first supported Cromwell, but they soon changed their minds. About 3,000 Parliamentary troops were billeted in the town and park, outnumbering the townspeople. Often the soldiers weren't paid, so they killed and ate the deer in the Great Park, even killing a gamekeeper who tried to stop them.

Trial and Execution

After three years, neither side had won. Parliament set up a New Model Army under Sir Thomas Fairfax. The soldiers were given scarlet uniforms and trained in Windsor Great Park. This new, trained army defeated the Royalists.

Charles I surrendered in 1646 and was held a prisoner while parliament attempted to reach an agreement with him. Charles was eventually charged with treason. He was found guilty and on 30th January, 1649 publicly executed at Whitehall. His body was brought to Windsor Castle on 7th February and he was buried two days later in a snowstorm.

The Commonwealth

The fighting caused damage to the town and the castle. After the king's death, Britain became a Commonwealth under Cromwell. He and his puritan followers had strict religious rules, wanting plain churches and services. They even forbade celebrating Christmas, which did not make them popular! But the Commonwealth did not survive long after Cromwell died in 1658.

The King Restored

Charles I's eldest son lived abroad after his father's defeat, but two years after Cromwell's death, he was asked to return as Charles II. The citizens of Windsor were delighted and the new king was proclaimed three times by trumpet: first at the Market House, next at the bridge, and finally at the castle gate. From then on, whenever he arrived in the town, the church bells were rung. He restored and rebuilt parts of the castle, restocked the park with deer, and created the Long Walk so that he could go hunting.

Can you spot this board which has been painted to reproduce the warrant and signatures for the king's execution? Look in Church Street.

Nell Gwyn, a popular actress, was given a house behind the castle so that she could meet Charles II easily.

Windsor's Guildhall

Windsor again grew as a wealthy market town. In 1687 the old Market House was demolished and a new one ordered by the Council. The old Guildhall was demolished too, so the new building took its place. It cost just over £2,000 (about £175,000 today) and was ready for use in 1690. The Guildhall was designed by Sir Thomas Fitch, but he died before it was finished. The Council asked the workmen to take any problems to Sir Christopher Wren, the architect of St Paul's Cathedral, who had connections with Windsor.

No one knows why there is a gap at the top of the central pillars under the Guildhall. But the room above has been used for meetings, banquets, balls and weddings ever since it was built – and the floor has never collapsed!

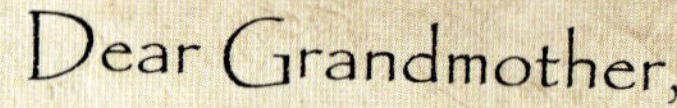

Sarah is a pupil at the Free School and they've just moved into their new building at the corner of the churchyard. In this imaginary account, she writes to her grandmother about it.

Dear Grandmother,

You bid me write you of my first day in the new school. Mr and Mrs Harwood welcomed us at the door. There's a bell outside which Mr Harwood will ring every morning when it's school-time. He says woe betide anyone coming in after the bell stops ringing! After saying prayers together, the girls stayed downstairs while the boys clomped upstairs to their classroom.

First we read the Bible story of Jonah being swallowed by the whale. I'd like to see a whale. Then we did writing. We older girls wrote out and learnt by heart the prayer for the day while Mrs Harwood taught the little ones to write their letters on scratchy slates. Next came accounting which I like least as I find sums dull.

For lunch we had a hunk of bread and a mug of ale, but for our first day we had a piece of cheese each too! Then in the afternoon we did sewing. I'm stitching shirts for new pupils when they come. I love school. I trust I will find a good position when I leave. I'd like to be a lady's maid as I'm good at sewing.

Your loving granddaughter,

Sarah

The Free School building still stands in Church Lane. If you look at the side of the building, you can see the brick arch where the school bell once hung.

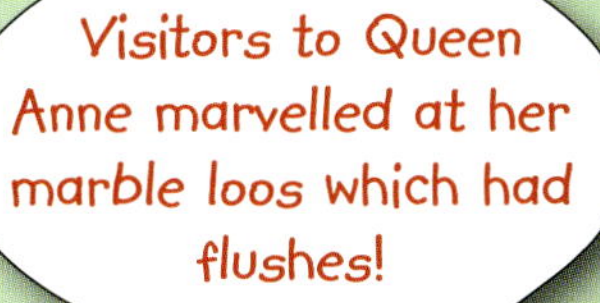

A view of Windsor from the meadows by Pieter Van der Aa in 1707.

How do we know?

In 1705 a 'free school' for poor children, 40 boys and 30 girls, was set up to teach them to 'read, write, cast accounts, and be well instructed in the principles of Religion'. Queen Anne gave £50 and her husband Prince George £30; altogether £201 was raised to start it off. At first the pupils met in the church, but in 1724 Theodore Randue left £500 to build a brick school building.

The children were chosen from poor, church-going families. Everything was provided for them: clothes, books and food. The girls wore smocks and mob caps and the boys breeches and caps. Even children drank weak beer then as water was too polluted. In 1725 the master's name was James Harwood, and it is likely that the mistress was his wife. They lived in the building. It was later known as the Royal Free School and though it moved and changed the school continued until 2000.

When Charles I's coffin was discovered in 1813 the decapitated head still had a reddish beard attached.

The Squire of Windsor

'Hey boy!' calls the big man. 'Knight's son, eh?' The boy makes the biggest bow he can. He's seen the figure approaching through the dewy fields, and knows it is the King, who's often been in his father's bookshop. The King peers into Charles's basket. 'Mushrooms eh? Tasty fried in butter, what what?' Charles wonders if he should hand them over, after all these are his fields. But the King pats him on the back, says he's a good lad, then strides off towards the castle.

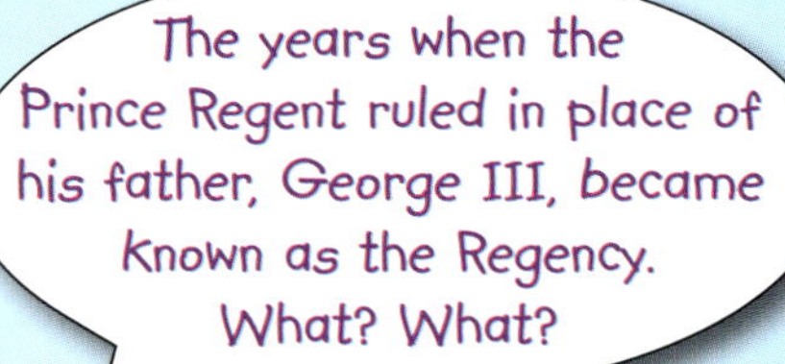

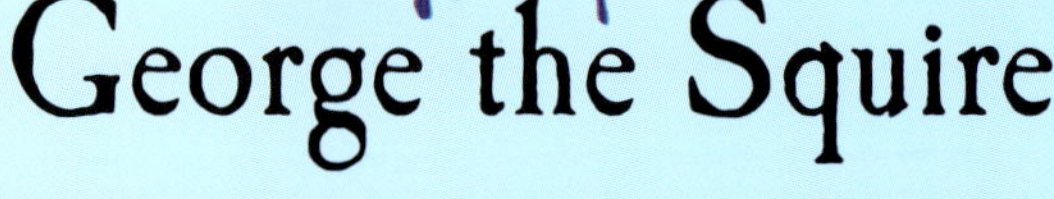

George the Squire

In Windsor the King lived more like a country squire than a king. He was nicknamed 'Farmer George' because he kept three farms in the Great Park. He loved to hunt too, chasing stags with names like Moonshine and Highflyer, which weren't killed but caught and kept for another day.

The King supported Eton College, and his birthday, 4th June, is still celebrated by the school. He visited Windsor shops and encouraged children to fly kites and play cricket or football in the park. On summer evenings a band would play on the castle terrace while he paraded with his family, chatting with the local people.

This painting shows George III returning from hunting in Windsor Great Park in the 1780s.

Hard Times

Life became difficult in the later years of George III's reign. War with Napoleon in France meant higher taxes, and the cost of bread rose, hitting the poor hard. There was a bread riot in 1800.

In 1812, Charles Knight and his father founded a weekly newspaper, *The Windsor Express*. It brought the town important news such as the defeat of Napoleon in the Battle of Waterloo in 1815. It also printed bulletins on the King's health. He had grown old and confused. All his farm stock was sold and his son took over from him as Prince Regent. But he was not forgotten: when he died in 1820 the newspaper had black borders and 30,000 people came to his funeral.

Windsor Town Bridge was made of cast iron, a new building material.

How do we know?

Charles Knight, a publisher and writer, wrote a book called *Passages of a Working Life*. In it he describes George III as a 'gossiping and inquiring gentleman' who often ended every sentence with 'What? what?' But he was well liked and when he recovered from a serious illness the town celebrated with a firework display.

Knight also records his father in 1800 calming bread rioters who came to smash the windows of the bakery next door to their bookshop on Castle Hill. The baker hid his money in the back bedroom.

New Look Windsor

In the 1820s, Windsor had a new parish church and a new bridge. Until 1898, tolls had to be paid by carriages crossing over the top and boats underneath. Barges delivered goods up and down the Thames, and in Windsor, they collected barrels of beer from the breweries by the riverside. George IV also spent a lot of money improving the castle. By raising the height of the Round Tower by half he changed its appearance for ever.

Can you spot the Copper Horse, a statue of George III dressed as a Roman Emperor, put up by George IV in his memory? Look for it at the end of the Long Walk.

Steam Trains and Slums

It's 8 am on 6th October, 1849, and workers in the fields of Eton Wick look up startled at the sound of puffing. A steam engine is coming in a wide curve along a wooden viaduct from Slough. It chuffs over a metal bridge then, with a hiss of steam, comes to a stop in the new Windsor Central Station. Driver-engineer Isambard Kingdom Brunel jumps down smiling broadly. His Great Western Railway has brought the first railway train into Windsor.

The Railway Race

Two railway companies competed to bring trains to Windsor, the Great Western Railway (GWR) and the South-Western Railway (SWR). Both were fiercely opposed. Eton College argued that the boys would throw stones at the trains or catch them to play truant. Prince Albert, Queen Victoria's husband, objected to trains crossing royal land. But finally he made a deal that gave the royal family more privacy. The SWR agreed to build two new bridges, Victoria Bridge and Albert Bridge, and a road to Datchet and Old Windsor, so Albert could close the public roads which went through the park near the castle. In return the town was given the land on the riverside, Home Park, for recreation.

The SWR should have got to Windsor first, but its bridge over the Thames collapsed. Once Eton withdrew its opposition, Brunel's GWR worked at break-neck speed. Its service began in October 1849, two months before the SWR's, whose station wasn't ready for another two years.

Brunel's iron railway bridge carried two rail tracks when it was opened in 1849. Now it has only one.

Slum Houses

A whole street of slum houses, George Street, was demolished to build Central Station. But the people made homeless just crowded into other slums, especially around the Goswells. These houses had no toilets or running water. Deadly diseases such as cholera and typhoid fever were common. Conditions were so bad that almost half of all children born died before their 5th birthday.

Windsor was a garrison town with two army barracks, the infantry and the cavalry, but living conditions were just as poor. Soldiers had to have permission to marry and their wives and children lived with them in a communal barrack room with only a sheet hung up for privacy.

By 1847, conditions in Windsor were so bad that it was suggested the town should be knocked down and rebuilt away from the Castle!

Prince Consort Cottages

Prince Albert worried about the bad housing of the poor and tried to improve matters. He and Victoria built modern homes and a school for their estate workers. The cottages were sturdily constructed, with good ventilation, running water, proper toilets and gardens. Sadly Windsor Castle's own drainage was as bad as the town's. Prince Albert himself caught typhoid fever and died in 1861.

Prince Consort Cottages, built in 1855, are still lived in today.

But I don't want to go to school!

Windsor Schools

Victoria and Albert had nine children, but royal children didn't go to school; they had tutors and governesses. For town children, there were church schools and one run by the army. Stephen Hawtrey, a clergyman, paid for two schools out of his own pocket – St Mark's for boys and St Anne's for girls. Parents paid a few pennies a week. For those who couldn't afford even that, a free 'Ragged School' was set up by a chimney-sweep concerned about boys who climbed the sooty chimneys to clean them. At first the school was held in a shed in George Street, but in 1854 it moved to a proper schoolhouse on Oxford Road. To celebrate, 150 of the poorest boys and girls were treated to coffee and cakes.

SP**O**T THIS!

Can you spot this date on a wall along with the initials PA (for Prince Albert) and VR (Victoria Regina)? Look around Riverside Station.

Rich Children, Poor Children

Edie scurries along the corridor, knowing she shouldn't be here. But her mother who dusts the royal drawing-room has told her about a beautiful tree put up for Christmas and she wants to see it. She can't hear any sounds in the room, so she turns the handle and slips in. She gasps amazed at the fir tree covered with candles. They flicker and glow, with shiny decorations hanging from the branches. Then a clear little voice asks,

'Who are you?' There's another, younger girl, who she instantly realizes must be a princess.

'Please,' she falters, 'I'm Edie. I'm very sorry but I wanted to see the tree.'

'I'm Alice,' replies the little girl. 'You can see it with me. Papa made it.' She takes Edie's hand and the two girls stand gazing at the marvellous tree together.

In 1848, the London Illustrated News published a picture showing Queen Victoria and Prince Albert with their tree and five of their six children: Vicky (8 years-old), Bertie (7), Alice (5), Affie (4), Helena (2). Prince Albert made the German Christmas tree tradition popular in England.

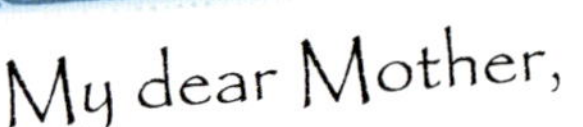

My dear Mother,

Here I am, sitting in my bedroom after the fatigues of the day... We sleep 4 together in one room. We lay in bed until 7.30 when a bell rings and we jump up and put trousers, slippers, socks and jacket on and hurry down and dust the shop... About 8.15 we hurry upstairs and dress and wash for breakfast. At 8.30 we go into a sort of vault underground (lit by gas) and have breakfast. I am in the shop and desk until dinner at 1 and then work until tea and then go on to supper at 8.30 at which time work is done. I don't like the place much for it is not at all like home.

Give love to Dad and give the cats my best respects.

Yours,
H. G. Wells

In 1880 a law made school compulsory for children up to the age of 10. Many parents couldn't afford to keep all their children at school and wanted them to get jobs. These often involved long hours at work. This extract from a real letter was written by 14-year-old Bertie (Herbert George) Wells in July 1880. He was an apprentice at Rodgers & Denyer, a grand draper's shop selling cloth in the High Street.

The master and boys of St Mark's School band pose with their instruments in 1863.

Poor children queue outside the bread shop for yesterday's stale bread in the 1890s.

A maid and the children in her care watch the foot guards marching past the old Victoria Barracks in Sheet Street in the 1890s.

How do we know?

We can find out about the arrival of the railways in Windsor, and the squabbling that went on, from council minutes, newspaper reports and parliamentary proceedings.

Most schools kept hand-written logbooks which noted day-to-day events, including punishments showing which boys were caned and for what.

H.G.Wells, later famous for stories such as 'The War of the Worlds', included the letter opposite in his autobiography. He lasted only a few weeks at Rodgers & Denyer. He hated it so much he used to hide in the basement and was soon sacked.

War, Flood, Frost and Fire

Friday 1st September, 1939: Throughout the day trains arrive at Riverside Station. Onto the platforms pour children labelled with their names, each carrying a gas-mask and a small suitcase. They've been evacuated from London to escape the threat of bombing. They're given 'ration' packs of biscuits, bully beef, tinned milk and chocolate. Then they are taken into Windsor or to nearby villages where they'll be living during the war.

Evacuees

On 3rd September, 1939, Britain declared war with Germany and World War Two began. Over three days about 9,000 children arrived by train to stay in homes which had volunteered to look after them and go to the local schools. It was strange, frightening and, of course, some of the evacuees were homesick. One young boy who missed his mum and dad roller-skated about 50 kilometres to Poplar in east London, then skated back next day.

Sidney Camm, a Windsor man, designed the Hurricane fighter-plane which helped win the war.

The German Messerschmitt crashed in the Great Park. Princesses Elizabeth and Margaret, who lived at Windsor Castle during the war, went to see the plane wreck which was put on show in Park Street.

Windsor at War

During the war, there was food rationing and other shortages as well as bombing. Nine people were killed and 111 injured during 40 air raids. Three doodlebug bombs fell on Windsor and Old Windsor causing two deaths. In 1940, a Messerschmitt fighter-plane crashed in the Great Park. The pilot, who wasn't injured, was taken prisoner. He spoke good English and asked politely for a cigarette.

Flood

Flooding has always been a problem in Windsor. In March 1947, the lower part of the town was under water for three weeks. The army brought in amphibious vehicles to rescue people and pets trapped in their houses or to take supplies to those who refused to leave. The postman delivered letters to upstairs rooms on the end of a long pole! The Jubilee River was created in 2002 to avoid a similar disaster.

Can you spot the name and badge of the regiment of the soldiers guarding Windsor Castle? Look outside Victoria Barracks on Sheet Street.

Datchet Green (above), Clewer, Eton and Windsor were badly hit during the floods of 1947.

Frost

Sometimes the Thames freezes over and skating is possible. In 1963 the landlord of the Bells of Ouzeley at Old Windsor served champagne on the ice, but a boy who proudly told his mum he'd crossed the river on foot to the Brocas was told off for being reckless.

Fire at the Castle

Around 11.30 am on 20th November, 1992 a woman ran into St George's Hall screaming 'Fire! Fire!' A curtain in the private chapel was on fire (probably ignited by a spotlight). Workmen grabbed fire extinguishers but could not put out the flames. Within half an hour fire had spread in all directions. The army, called to rescue precious works of art, formed human chains to pass objects from one to another. The Queen and members of the royal family helped. Despite fire engines racing to the scene from all over Berkshire the fire raged on. That evening the people of Windsor watched, horrified, as the Brunswick Tower exploded into flame like a gigantic firework. It took until the following morning to extinguish the blaze, leaving grand rooms smouldering in ruins.

After painstaking repairs, Windsor Castle reopened to visitors just five years after the fire, in 1997.

Windsor Today and Tomorrow

We can't know everything about the past, but we can learn a great deal from archaeological digs, documents, maps, old letters, pictures, photographs, newspapers and nowadays films and recordings. We know what the town is like today – but what will people in the future find?

The changing of the guard always draws crowds of spectators. But will there still be kings and queens to protect in a hundred years time?

Eton College is the most famous school in the world. Princes William and Harry were both at Eton and several prime ministers have been educated at the school. Will the pupils still wear tail-coats in the future?

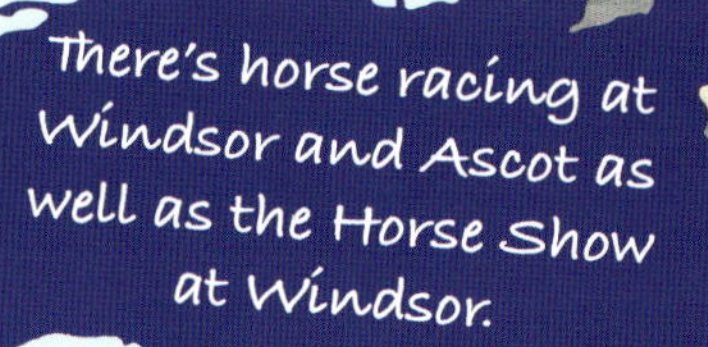

There's horse racing at Windsor and Ascot as well as the Horse Show at Windsor.

Windsor Castle has more than a million visitors a year.

The River Thames is used for pleasure cruises but if roads become too crowded could it once again become an important highway to carry goods?

Legoland attracts thousands of tourists every year. What will the plastic brick models show for future visitors to see?

...2002 *Jubilee River* named in honour of *Elizabeth II's Golden Jubilee*...

When the Queen stays at Windsor Castle the Royal Standard flies above the Round Tower.

Can you spot this plaque? Look inside the Leisure Centre.

The old Fire Station is now an Arts Centre.

How will they know?

Today we can find out much of what we want to know from the internet. But will such information still be there in a hundred years time? We don't write letters as people did in the past, but we send emails or talk to our friends on mobile phones leaving no permanent record. When future historians want to know what life was like for us will today's Facebook and social networking sites still be available? Perhaps in a thousand years there will be archaeologists digging in our rubbish pits to find out what our lives were like just as we do for the lives of people in the distant past.

Market Cross House, known as the Crooked House, was first built in 1592, but rebuilt in 1718.

Glossary

AD – a short way of writing the Latin words anno Domini, which mean 'in the year of our Lord' (after the birth of Christ).

Amphibious – a vehicle that can move on land or water.

Amphitheatre – an open-air theatre with rows of seats one above the other.

Apprentice – someone learning a trade.

Archaeologist – a person who studies the past by uncovering the remains of buildings and digging up objects from the ground.

BC – a short way of writing 'before the birth of Christ'.

Billeted – ordered to live somewhere.

Bully beef – tinned meat.

Catholic – a member of the Christian religion that considers the Pope to be the head of its church.

Charter – a document which grants rights to a borough.

Chivalry – the rules for how knights should behave.

Commonwealth – government by the people.

Crown-wearing – a ceremony where the king shows himself to his people wearing his crown.

Evacuee – a person sent away from home to a safe place during war to avoid bombing.

Garrison – a place where soldiers (troops) are stationed.

Garter – a band of cloth used to hold up stockings.

Heretic – someone who holds beliefs which are not acceptable to the majority of people.

Keep – a tower which forms a castle stronghold.

Kirtle – a knee-length tunic.

Latin – a language originally spoken in Ancient Rome.

Lists – the area in which medieval jousts take place.

Medieval – the period of time between the Anglo-Saxons and the Tudors. The word means 'Middle Ages'.

Parliamentarian – anyone who fought on the side of Parliament against Charles I in the English Civil War.

Patron – a protector and supporter.

Pillory - a wooden frame with holes for the head and hands, used for punishment.

Prince Consort – the title given to Prince Albert, husband of Queen Victoria.

Puritan – a person of strict views about the Christian Church.

Royal Charter – written permission from the king or queen.

Royal Standard – the flag used by Queen Elizabeth II.

Royalist – anyone who fought on the side of King Charles I in the English Civil War.

Sacrament – a Christian ceremony.

Siege – surrounding or blockading a place to try and capture it.

Toll – a fee paid to cross a bridge or use a road.

Trenchers – thick rounds of bread used as plates in medieval times.

Visors – part of a helmet, covering and protecting the face of a knight.

Index

Acknowledgements

The author and publishers would like to thank the following people for their generous help:
Elias Kupfermann, Brigitte Mitchell, Andrew Fielder, Pamela Marson, all of the Windsor Local History Group; Margaret Kirby, Caroline McCutcheon and the team at Windsor Museum; Steven Archer and the London Library

The publishers would like to thank the following people and organizations
for their permission to reproduce material on the following pages:
p5: Windsor & Royal Borough Museum; p6: Windsor & Royal Borough Museum; p7: Windsor & Royal Borough Museum; p8: The Windsor Guide, Charles Knight Sr, 1793; p9: Windsor & Royal Borough Museum; Magna-Tagishsimon at en.wikipedia; Pamela Marson; p10: Lampman/Wikipedia; Sodacan-wikipedia; p11: Dawn Fielder, Copperhorse Publishing; p12: Annals of Windsor, Tighe and Davis, 1858; p13: Stefano Bianchetti/Corbis; p14: The Pictorial Edition of the Works of Shakespere, ed by Charles Knight, 1867; Hart & Garter Hotel, Windsor; p17: Doug Harding; Hester Davenport; p19: La Delice de la Grande Bretagne, James Beverell, 1707, supplied by Elias Kupfermann; p20: James Pollard/gettyimages; p21: Hester Davenport; p24: Illustrated London News Ltd/Mary Evans; p25: Record Office for Leicestershire, Leciester and Rutland; p26: Windsor Express; p27: Windsor & Royal Borough Museum; Martin Beddall/Alamy; p28: Hester Davenport; www.legoland.co.uk

All other images copyright of Hometown World

Every effort has been made to trace and acknowledge the ownership of copyright.
If any rights have been omitted, the publishers offer to rectify this in any future editions.

Written by Hester Davenport
Educational consultant: Neil Thompson
Local history consultant: Brigitte Mitchell
Designed by Stephen Prosser

Illustrated by Kate Davies, Dynamo Ltd, Virginia Gray, Peter Kent, John McGregor, Tim Sutcliffe
Additional photographs by Alex Long

First published by HOMETOWN WORLD in 2011
Hometown World Ltd
7 Northumberland Buildings
Bath BA1 2JB

www.hometownworld.co.uk

Copyright © Hometown World Ltd 2011

hb ISBN 978-1-84993-132-8
pb ISBN 978-1-84993-156-4

Your **past**
Your **now**
Your **future**

Your **history4ever**

My next one's going to have 2 wheels!

I love you too!